EDGE BOOKS™

W9-ARB-283

Stunning STAGE TRICKS

by Norm Barnhart

CAPSTONE PRESS
a capstone imprint

Edge Books are published by Capstone Press,
1710 Roe Crest Drive, North Mankato, Minnesota 56003
www.capstonepub.com

Copyright © 2014 by Capstone Press, a Capstone imprint. All rights reserved.
No part of this publication may be reproduced in whole or in part, or stored in a
retrieval system, or transmitted in any form or by any means, electronic, mechanical,
photocopying, recording, or otherwise, without written permission of the publisher.

Library of Congress Cataloging-in-Publication Data
Barnhart, Norm.
Stunning stage tricks / by Norm Barnhart.
pages cm.—(Edge books. Magic manuals)
Includes bibliographical references.
Summary: "Step-by-step instructions and photos show how to do a variety of fun
and entertaining stage illusions"—Provided by publisher.
ISBN 978-1-4765-0135-2 (library binding)
ISBN 978-1-4765-3391-9 (ebook PDF)
1. Tricks—Juvenile literature. I. Title.
GV1548.B366 2014
793.8—dc23   2013004940

Editorial Credits
Aaron Sautter, editor; Tracy Davies McCabe, designer; Svetlana Zhurkin,
media researcher; Jennifer Walker, production specialist; Sarah Schuette,
photo stylist; Marcy Morin, photo scheduler

Photo Credits
All interior photos by Capstone Studio/Karon Dubke.
Cover and background images by Shutterstock/Gl0ck, L. Watcharapol, Max Blain,
Merydolla, Molodec, and simonekesh.

Printed in the United States of America in Stevens Point, Wisconsin.
032013   007227WZF13

TABLE OF CONTENTS

STUPENDOUS STAGE MAGIC

Illusions performed on stage are often the most amazing of all magic tricks. World-famous magician David Copperfield leaves people in awe of his grand illusions. He is known for making huge objects disappear and making people float in midair. Practice the illusions in this book, and soon you'll also be wowing the crowd with your incredible magical skills!

SETTING THE STAGE

Stage magic often requires some special preparation. Follow these steps to make your tricks seem effortless and exciting.

Blocking: Plan out and practice where you and your assistants will stand and move during the show. Be sure everybody knows where to be at the proper time.

Lighting: Lights help set the mood for your tricks. If you do a spooky trick, use dim lighting.

Music: Music is another way to help set the mood for an audience. It can also cover up the sound of someone moving around off stage.

Magic Secret: Assistants

Stage illusions often require the help of assistants. Ask a few friends if they'd like to be your assistants. With their help, you'll soon be mastering the tricks in this book.

On-Stage Assistants

On-stage assistants work with magicians on the stage. They are often involved with the secrets behind illusions. Stage assistants dress sharp, smile a lot, and follow the magician's lead on the stage.

Secret Assistants

Secret assistants hide behind a curtain or under a table and wait to do their part of a trick. They stay very quiet so they do not give away their location. Some secret assistants pretend to be part of the audience and volunteer when needed.

Dr. Freeze

With an icy stare, Dr. Freeze can zap water into ice. People will gasp when they see you instantly change water into frozen ice cubes!

What You Need:
- 2 paper cups
- 1 kitchen sponge
- scissors
- glass of water
- ice cubes

PREPARATION:

1. Cut a circle from the sponge that fits snugly in the bottom of one cup. Place the sponge circle into the cup.

2. Just before the show, put three ice cubes into the cup.

PERFORMANCE:

1. Place the cup and a glass of water on the table. Tell the audience, "I once met a scientist named Dr. Freeze. He taught me this really cool trick."

2. Pour a bit of water from the glass into the cup. Hold up the cup and say, "Dr. Freeze just gave the water a cold, icy stare—like this." Face the cup and give it a cold, hard stare.

6

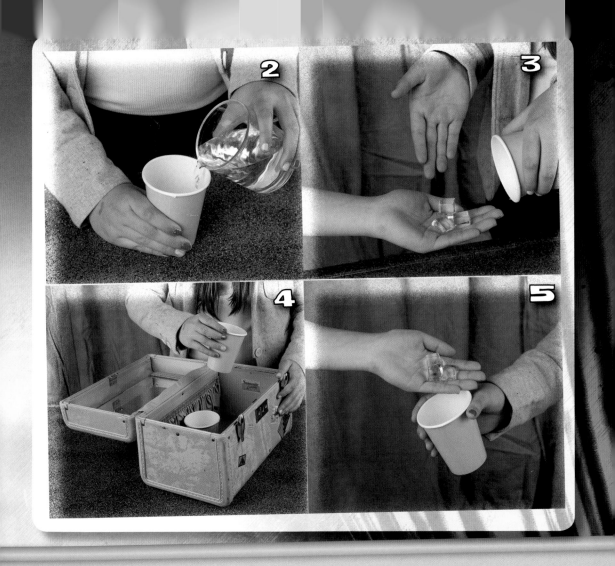

3. Ask for a volunteer from the audience. Have the volunteer hold out his or her hands. Turn the cup over and dump the ice cubes into the volunteer's hands.

4. Ask the volunteer to walk into the audience and show the ice cubes to another person. As the volunteer does this, casually place the cup in your magic case and secretly grab the second cup. Ask the volunteer to come back to the stage. Then say, "You probably don't want to hold onto that ice very long."

5. Ask the volunteer to place the ice cubes in the new cup. Then say, "Dr. Freeze also showed me a second part to this trick. It's called the 'melting ice' trick. But it takes a lot longer. We'll check the ice at the end of the show to see if it worked." The audience will get a laugh from this joke because they know the ice will just melt normally.

Super Magno Man

How would you like to be a superhero with amazing magnetic powers? Your friends' jaws will drop when they see crayons, newspaper, and even a rubber ball magically stick to your fingers!

What You Need:

- magician's gloves
- several small magnets
- tape
- small nails
- a crayon
- a rubber ball
- a sheet of newspaper
- a small metal washer
- a table

PREPARATION:

1. Turn one glove inside out. Tape magnets inside the first two fingers of the glove. Then turn it right side out.

2. Push a small nail into the end of the crayon.

3. Push a few nails into the rubber ball. Make sure the heads of the nails are flat with the surface of the ball.

4. Tape the small washer into a corner of the newspaper.

PERFORMANCE:

1. Set out the prepared objects and the gloves. Ask the audience, "Have you ever wished you could have super powers like the heroes in comic books?" Put on the gloves, then say, "I discovered I have a super power of my own. When I rub my hands together, some sort of magnetic force builds up."

2. Push the crayon around with the non-magnetic hand. It will move but doesn't stick. Then rub your hands together and act like you are building up a magnetic force.

3. Tap the crayon with the magnetic hand. The crayon will stick to your fingers and start to lift from the table. Hold it up so the audience can see it hanging from your fingertips.

4. Repeat steps 2 and 3 with the rubber ball.

5. Repeat steps 2 and 3 with the newspaper. Crumple the newspaper into a ball before using the magnetic glove on it.

6. Tell the audience, "I plan to start my own comic hero based on my powers. He'll be called Super Magno Man. Maybe there will be a movie about him someday!"

TRICK THREE
FLOATING ASSISTANT

Making a person float in the air is a classic illusion. With a little practice, you'll leave your audience in awe when your assistant seems to magically rise into the air.

What You Need:

- one large cardboard box
- paint or markers
- a bench
- a tablecloth
- scissors
- two sets of matching shoes that fit assistant
- two pairs of matching pants that fit assistant
- two sticks, 4-feet (1.2-meters) long
- hammer and nails
- a magic wand
- an assistant

PREPARATION:

1. Cut the cardboard box and decorate it to look like a large book. Add a fun title and author like "How to Fly: by the Wrong Brothers."

2. Attach one pair of shoes to the sticks with nails. Place one pair of pants over the wood sticks to create fake legs.

3. Place a bench on the stage and cover it with the tablecloth. Make sure the tablecloth reaches to the floor. Place the fake legs behind the bench. Have your assistant wear the matching set of shoes and pants.

11

TIP: This trick depends on smooth movements by the assistant. Be sure to practice this trick several times before performing it.

PERFORMANCE:

1. Hold up the cardboard book to show the audience. Tell them, "I recently found this incredible book. It says you don't need a plane to fly. You just need to use a little magic. Let's give it a try."

2. Ask your assistant to lie down on the bench. Place the book in front of her as shown (2a). As you do this, she will place the fake legs on the bench behind the book. The assistant's feet will stay on the floor (2b). The audience should now see the assistant's head and the fake legs on the bench behind the book (2c).

3. Now slowly wave your magic wand over your assistant. As you do this, she will slowly raise the fake legs and begin to sit up at the same time (3a). This motion creates the illusion that the assistant is floating above the bench (3b).

4. The assistant then slowly lowers the fake legs and lies back down. Step to the side to remove the book. As you do this, your assistant will secretly place the fake legs out of view behind the bench.

5. Take away the book and help your assistant stand up. Thank her for helping you. Then have her take a bow and ask the audience to give her a round of applause.

TRICK FOUR
THE TELEPORTING BUNNY

Silly rabbit—you'll be late for the show! Your audience won't believe it when they see a rabbit vanish from its dressing room and reappear in the magic hat.

What You Need:
- two identical stuffed toy rabbits
- a large hat
- a shoebox
- scissors
- paint or markers
- a magic case

PREPARATION:

1. Cut a secret hole in the back of the hat large enough to fit your fingers. Place the two stuffed rabbits into the hat.

2. Cut a flap in the bottom of the shoebox to make a secret trap door. Be sure to make it large enough to fit one stuffed rabbit through. Color the box to look like an actor's dressing room.

PERFORMANCE:

1. Bring out the hat using both hands. As you pick it up, slip your fingers into the secret hole to hold one rabbit in place (1a). Hold up the hat for the audience and say, "I'd like you to meet my friend Harry." (1b).

2. Tip the hat toward you and drop the second rabbit into your free hand. Tipping the hat toward you keeps the first rabbit hidden from the audience. Hold the second rabbit up and show it to the audience. Say, "Harry is a great pet, but he likes to take naps in my hat."

3. Put the hat and secret hidden rabbit on your head. Make sure the secret hole is facing away from the audience.

4. Pretend to talk to the first rabbit and say, "OK Harry, nap time is over. It's time to go to your room and get ready for the show." Take out the shoebox and place it on the edge of your magic case. Pretend to place the rabbit in the shoebox (4a). You will actually slide the rabbit through the secret trap door to let it drop into the magic case (4b).

5. Put the top on the box and pick it up. Pretend to talk to the rabbit inside. Talk about how the bunny is always late for the show. After doing this for a little while, stop and pretend to listen to the box. Ask, "Harry, are you ready yet?"

6. Open the shoebox and look inside. Then give the audience a surprised look. Tip the box over to show them that the rabbit is gone!

7. Put the box down and pick up your magic wand. Say, "I can't believe he did this again! Harry tries to use magic sometimes. But he always gets stuck." Wave the wand at the box and say some magic words. As you do this, pretend you feel something moving on your head.

8. Take off the hat to show the rabbit hiding under it. Say, "Harry! How many times have I said not to use magic? Time to go back to your room." Place the rabbit inside the box and put it back in your magic case.

Rainbow Hanky

What do you do if you need a handkerchief? Make your own! Your audience can join the fun with this trick as you make a colorful hanky magically appear.

What You Need:

- two sheets of newspaper
- a large, colorful hanky
- glue
- a magic wand

PREPARATION:

1. Lay one sheet of newspaper flat on a table. Place the hanky on top of it.

2. Spread a thin layer of glue along the outside edge of the newspaper.

3. Place the second sheet of newspaper on top. Line up the edges so it looks like a single sheet of paper. Press the two sheets together and allow the glue to dry.

PERFORMANCE:

1. Pretend you are about to sneeze and need a handkerchief. Pretend to search your pockets for a hanky. Tell the audience, "I must have left my hanky at home. I need your help to make another one."

2. Take out the prepared newspaper and show both sides to the audience (2a). Then crumple it into a ball. Look into the audience and find someone wearing a red shirt. Point to that person and say, "Could you pinch off a bit of red dust from your shirt and toss it toward me?" Then pretend to catch the red "dust" and put it in the newspaper (2b).

3. Ask the audience, "Does anyone have any green or purple?" Ask more people to toss bits of colorful dust from their shirts toward the paper. Repeat this step for as many colors as you wish.

4. Take out your magic wand and wave it at the paper (4a). Make a small tear in the paper to grab the hidden handkerchief. Quickly pull the colorful hanky out of the newspaper and show it to the audience (4b). Tell the crowd, "Thanks for your help. This should come in handy!" Then pretend to sneeze using the new hanky.

Instant Vacation

Making a person disappear into thin air is a classic illusion. Audiences are always stunned when someone vanishes in a flash. Here is one secret to performing this amazing trick.

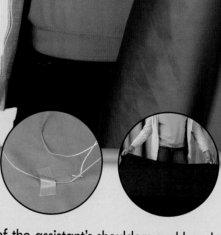

What You Need:

- an assistant
- a large colorful bed sheet
- 16-gauge solid wire, 8 feet (2.4 meters) long
- tape
- a table
- black cloth
- a tropical shirt, sunglasses, and a hat

PREPARATION:

1. Bend the wire into a frame in the shape of the assistant's shoulders and head. Tape the wire frame into the colorful sheet.

2. Cover the table with enough black cloth so it reaches the floor. The audience should not be able to see under the table. Place the covered table on the stage near the back curtain. Place the prepared sheet on the floor behind the table.

> TIP: Try adding some comedy to the end of this trick by having the assistant put on a winter coat and hat instead of the tropical clothes. Then he or she can act mad about being sent to the South Pole instead of Hawaii.

PERFORMANCE:

1. Ask your assistant to step forward and stand next to the table. Tell the audience that your assistant has always been very helpful. Tell them that you want to send her on a magical vacation trip. Ask her where she'd like to go. She should say that she's always wanted to visit Hawaii.

2. Say, "OK! Hawaii it is. Get ready for the trip of a lifetime!" Lift up the sheet to hide the assistant from the audience (2a). Then pretend to wrap the sheet around her. The wire frame should be at the top to look like her head and shoulders (2b).

3. During this process the assistant will crouch down and hide behind the table. She will then sneak out through the curtain behind the table.

4. Next, grab the wire frame with both hands and pretend to help the "covered assistant" walk to the front of the stage. Practice this step ahead of time to make it seem real for the audience. Say, "Are you ready for your vacation?" Pretend that the assistant whispers something to you (4a). Say, "Don't worry, this won't hurt a bit!" As you perform this part, the assistant secretly puts on the tropical clothes behind the curtain (4b).

5. Say some magic words like "Pippity, Poppity, Pop!" Then whisk away the sheet with both hands to show that the assistant has instantly vanished!

6. Take a bow as the audience applauds. As you do this, the assistant should walk onto the stage wearing the tropical clothes. Ask her how she enjoyed her vacation. She should say, "It was great! But it was awfully short." Have her take a bow and ask the crowd to give her a round of applause.

SUPER STRETCHO

Do you want a snack that's a bit out of reach? That's easy—just use the Super Stretcho Box! The audience will be surprised to see you grab a snack that is several feet away.

What You Need:
- a box about 4 feet (1.2 meters) long
- paint or markers
- two sets of identical gloves
- a bowl of potato chips
- an assistant

PREPARATION:

1. Cut a hole in each end of the box large enough to fit your arm through.

2. Cut another secret hole in the back of the box near one end.

3. Decorate the outside of the box to look like a magical device. Include the name "Super Stretcho" on the box.

4. Place a few chips inside the box. Place the bowl of chips on a table at one end of the stage.

5. Put on one pair of gloves. The assistant will also wear a glove on one hand.

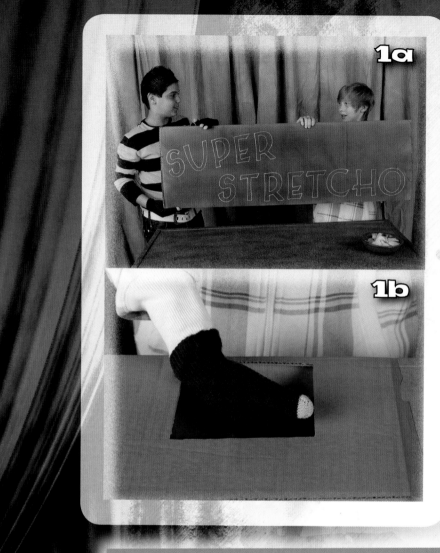

TIP: This trick can be repeated a few times to make the illusion seem real. The assistant should look surprised each time you eat a chip.

PERFORMANCE:

1. Walk onto the stage holding one end of the Super Stretcho box. Your assistant will hold the other end (1a). He or she will have one gloved hand inside the secret hole (1b). The assistant's other hand can be seen holding the box.

2. When you see the bowl of chips on the table say, "Hey, chips! I could use a snack." The assistant will say, "I can get them for you." Then say, "That's OK. I can reach them from here."

3. Reach into the box with one hand. After a moment, your assistant will reach his or her gloved hand through the secret hole and the other end of the box. It will look like your arm has stretched all the way through the box!

4. Your assistant will grab a chip from the bowl on the table and pull it back into the box. As this happens, you will grab one of the secret chips hidden inside the box.

5. Bring out your hand holding the chip. Give the audience a big smile and munch on the potato chip. As you eat the chip, the assistant will give the audience a stunned look. The assistant's surprised look will help the audience believe that you really stretched your arm through the box.

Astounding Card Appearance

Your audience will be speechless when you make cards appear from nowhere! First you make a single card appear. Then a whole handful of cards instantly appears out of thin air.

What You Need:
- nine playing cards
- two identical large handkerchiefs
- sewing thread and needle

PREPARATION:

1. Glue eight playing cards together to form a fan.

2. Sew the handkerchiefs together on three sides to make a secret pocket. Leave the fourth side open.

3. When dry, place the fan of cards into the secret pocket in the handkerchiefs. Keep the hanky and the ninth card in your magic case.

PERFORMANCE:

1. Take out the handkerchief and the single card. Hold the card between your first and second fingers behind your hand as shown to hide it from the audience. Hold up your hand to show the audience your empty palm.

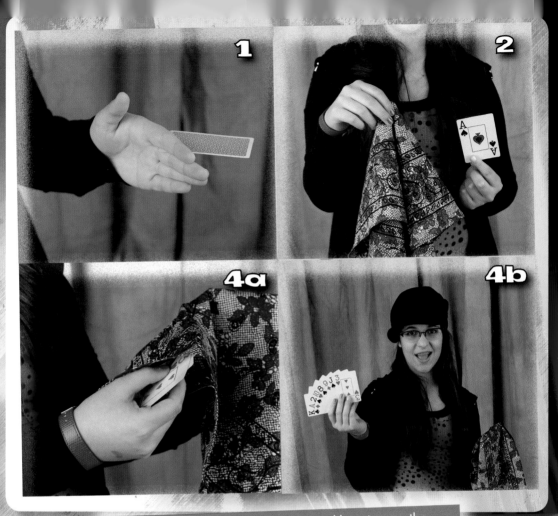

TIP: When finished with this trick, quickly put away the props and move on to your next trick. You will only be able to do this illusion once without giving away the secret.

2. Wave the handkerchief over your hand. As it covers your hand, flick the card up and hold it between your thumb and first finger. When you pull away the hanky, it will look as if the card appeared out of thin air.

3. Toss the card into the magic case. Then show the audience both sides of the hanky to show that it is empty. They won't see the secret fan of cards hidden inside.

4. Lay the hanky over your empty hand again. As you do this, secretly grab the hidden fan of cards (4a). Quickly pull the hanky away to show that the cards have magically appeared (4b).

THE LiViNG DOLL

In some stories, dolls wish they could be real. With this incredible illusion, you can make it happen. The audience will be stunned when this doll jumps out of the box as a real living person!

What You Need:

- a large cardboard appliance box
- extra cardboard
- scissors
- tape
- paint or markers
- a doll
- a costume that matches the doll's outfit
- an assistant

PREPARATION:

1. Create a dollhouse out of the large box. Cut a flap in the front to form the front door of the dollhouse.

2. Use an extra piece of cardboard to form a roof for the dollhouse.

3. Measure and cut another piece of cardboard to form a secret wall inside the dollhouse. Place the cardboard so it forms a secret space for your assistant to hide inside. Tape it in place on one side so it can swing like a door.

4. Use paint or markers to draw and color the box to look like a house. Then place the doll inside.

5. The assistant should wear clothes that match the doll's outfit.

6. Place the box on the stage before your show.

7. The assistant will hide in the secret space inside the box.

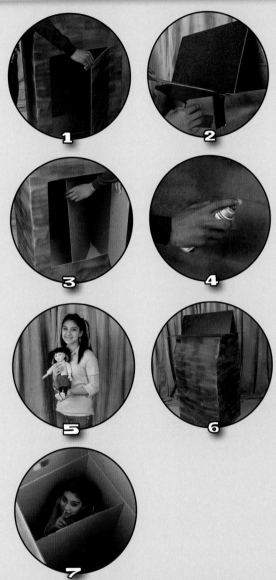

TIP: This trick should be performed at the beginning of your show. You don't want to make your assistant hide inside the box for a long time.

PERFORMANCE:

1. Walk onto the stage and begin telling the audience a story about the dollhouse. Stand next to the dollhouse and say, "I found this little house at a garage sale. The owner told me that it has special magical qualities."

2. Open the front door of the dollhouse to show there is only a doll inside. Take the doll out and show it to the audience. Say, "The house even came with its own doll. I don't know the doll's name, but the owner said she's lived here for a long time."

3. Place the doll back in the house and close the door. Tell the audience, "The owner said that if enough people clap three times and say the right magic word, something amazing happens!" Lead the audience to clap three times and shout the magic word "Pocuscadabra!"

4. As the crowd shouts the magic word, wave your hands toward the dollhouse in a magical way. At this point your assistant will pop through the front door of the dollhouse with a "Ta-da!" pose. It will look like the doll has suddenly come to life! Have your assistant step out of the box and take a bow. Then ask the audience to give her a round of applause as she leaves the stage.

READ MORE

Einhorn, Nicholas. *Stand-up Magic and Optical Illusions.* Inside Magic. New York: Rosen Central, 2011.

Schafer, Albert. *Illusionology: The Secret Science of Magic.* Somerville, Mass.: Candlewick Press, 2012.

Turnbull, Stephanie. *Incredible Illusions.* Secrets of Magic. Mankato, Minn.: Smart Apple Media, 2012.

INTERNET SITES

FactHound offers a safe, fun way to find Internet sites related to this book. All of the sites on FactHound have been researched by our staff.

Here's all you do:

Visit *www.facthound.com*

Type in this code: 9781476501352

 **Super-cool stuff!** Check out projects, games and lots more at **www.capstonekids.com**